Fish, Flies, and Fleas

by Dave Miller, Ph.D.

A.P. "Learn to Read" Series

God made fish.

I wish I had a fish.

I wish I had a dish of fish.

Do you like to eat fish?

Fish swim in lakes.

Fish swim in rivers.

Fish swim in the sea.

Fish swim in lakes, rivers, and the sea.

Fish have fins.

God made fish.

God made the fly.

The fly has big eyes.

A fly can fly.

A fly can get on food.

Shoo, fly! Shoo!

Get off of my food!

God made the fly.

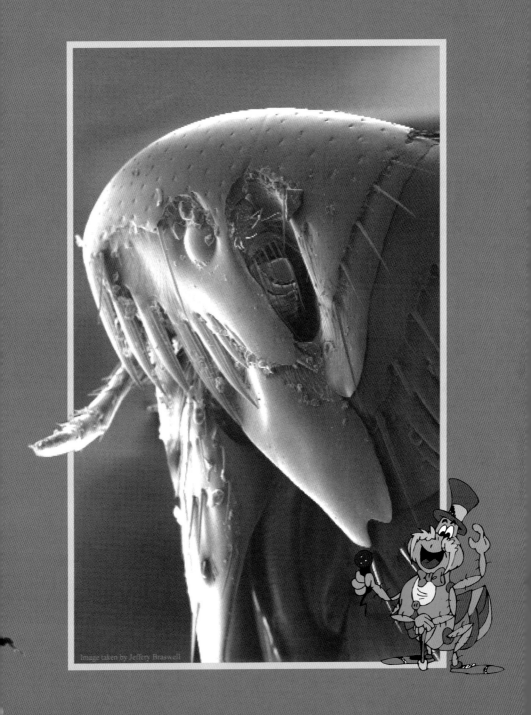

Image taken by Jeffery Braswell

God made the flea.

Fleas can get on dogs cats, and rats.

My dog has fleas.

Fleas make you itch.

God made the flea.

God made fish,
flies, and fleas.

God made them all.

God made them all on
days five and six.

God is good!

The "Learn to Read" Series: A Word to Parents

Rationale: To provide books for children (ages 3-6) from Christian homes for the purpose of assisting them in **learning to read** while simultaneously introducing them to the **Creator** and His **creation.**

Difficulty Level

The following listing provides a breakdown of the number and length of words in *Fish, Flies, and Fleas* (not counting plurals and duplicates):

Total Number of Words: 47

2—One letter words
I, a

7—Two letters words
do, in, is, my,
of, on, to

21—Three letter words
God, had, sea, dog, the, six,
fin, fly, has, cat, big, you,
eat, eye, can, rat, get,
off, and, all, day,

16—Four letter words
made, fish, wish, dish, make,
food, shoo, them, five, good,
like, lake, have, flea,
swim, itch

1—Five letter word
river

Drawings by
Kyrsti Dubcak, Age 8

The A.P. Readers

LEVEL 1
"Learn to Read"

1. Dogs, Frogs, and Hogs

2. Bats, Cats, and Rats

3. Birds, Bugs, and Bees

4. Fish, Flies, and Fleas

5. Goose, Moose, and Mongoose

6. Ducks, Bucks, and Woodchucks

LEVEL 2
"Early Reader"

1. God Made the World

2. God Made Dinosaurs

3. God Made Animals

4. God Made Insects

5. God Made Plants

6. God Made Fish

LEVEL 3
"Advanced Reader"

Coming Soon!

We are continuing to expand the number of titles in each series. Be sure to check our Web site for our newest books.
www.ApologeticsPress.org